I0517032

LEARNING TO LIVE FEAR

Free

LEON COLLIER

BLUEPRINT PRESS
INTERNATIONALE

Learning to Live Fear Free
Copyright © 2022 by Leon Collier

All rights reserved. No part of this publication may be reproduced, distributed, or transmitted in any form or by any means, including photocopying, recording, or other electronic or mechanical methods, without the prior written permission of the author, except in the case of brief quotations embodied in critical reviews and certain other non-commercial uses permitted by copyright law.

ISBN
978-1-957895-64-2 (Paperback)
978-1-957895-65-9 (eBook)

TABLE OF
CONTENTS

INTRODUCTION

Fear is a basic human instinct encoded into the nervous system, and from the time of our birth, we are armed with survival makeup when facing danger. When we detect danger, our neurological system quickly sends warning signals to the body, which causes bodily responses and blood pumps to muscle groups to prepare the body to run or defend.

It is in our human nature to fear, which came from sin. Fear did not exist in our human makeup until Adam sinned. The first occurrence of anxiety was in the Garden of Eden after Adam and Eve sinned. After they disobeyed God's command, you may recall that they ran and hid from the Lord in fear. "So, he said, "I heard your voice in the garden, and I was afraid because I was naked, and I hid myself" (Genesis 3:10, NKJV). Thus, living in fear does not originate with God. It comes from sin and disobedience to God. The Spirit of fear lies within the human biological structure and flares up at the rise of potential danger. But when we accepted Christ, He gave us another spirit that can combat the spirit of fear, and that spirit is the spirit of power, love, and sound mind. We have miraculous working power in us to change unfavorable circumstances into favorable ones. We also have agape love that casts out fear (1 John 4:18) and a sound mind that helps keep us under the Holy Spirit's control, which is how God expects His people to live in this imperfect world where tragedy can happen unexpectedly at any given time.

Based on my research, the word fear is mentioned 395 times in the Bible. God understands how imperfect humans live in an imperfect world where so many unexpected tragedies can happen to make room for the temptation to live in fear. The word fear is mentioned so frequently because it is a real issue in the world.

Interestingly, the phrase "fear not" is only found 63 times in the Bible based on my research. If fear is mentioned 365 times, fear not is only mentioned 63 times in the Bible; perhaps God didn't have to say fear not as much because He had a remedy for it.

Satan makes a lot of noise like a roaring lion, and he intends to frighten you and suppress your faith, but remember you are a child of God, and Satan is a lion with no teeth and no claws. Satan may catch you off guard at first because your brain has to catch up with your physical response to the instant threat but always remember with God, threats are nothing more than a shadow of death, as stated so eloquently by King David (Psalm 23:4). We can deal with our fears, or we can run. People tend to shun the things they fear, but this doesn't help them conquer fear. It fortifies fear. This is why I felt inspired to write about fear so that Christians can learn to live fear-free.

People often live with unnecessary phobias due to bad experiences. A part of our brain (amygdala) records our experiences of tragedies that prompt intense emotions when we think about them. Phobias are not evil; they are simply a reaction our minds have adapted to warn and protect us.

Some phobias are false alarms because there is no real threat. Humans often psychologically exacerbate situations when they are not as critical as perceived, of which the Lord wants us to be cognizant. We have Him who has all power, and therefore, the perceived threat is not as significant as we make it. David and Goliath are prime examples. Goliath was a giant and stood head and shoulders above the young teenage boy, David, but his God was more prominent than Goliath and certainly more powerful.

We experience types of fear regularly, such as failure. Our society is success-driven which primes and prompts us to be winners at all costs, but God has a different view of success than the world. The world's definition of success is money, power, and positions, but God's idea of success is faithful service. One of our greatest fears is the fear of death. People fear death because they are not sure what lies beyond this life which is why our society fights so hard to stay young. Of course, death is not negative if you are on the right side of the fence. The Bible says, "...to be absent from the body, and to be at home with the Lord." (2 Corinthians 5:8 WEB)

Some people fear commitment produced by a lack of trust stemming from heartbreak, and their distrust serves as a buffer to avoid such. The heart is the softest spot in human emotions, and it is the most vulnerable. You can't tell your heart what to do because it is independent and will deceive you if given a chance, according to Jeremiah 17:9. The heart is always up for grabs to avail itself of opportunities to gratify its corrupt proclivities. We can guard our hearts by prayer (Philippians 4:6, 7).

As we learn how to live fear-free, we will use the teaching of our Savior, Jesus Christ, the Prince of Peace, and ultimate instructor on this subject.

CHAPTER 1

Things that can provoke fear in us

In Matthew chapter ten, Jesus mentioned the word fear four times.

#1 Matthew 10:26, "Therefore do not fear them. For there is nothing covered that will not be revealed and hidden that will not be known."

#2-3 Matthew 10:28, "Do not fear those who kill the body but cannot kill the soul. But rather fear Him who can destroy both soul and body in hell."

#4 Matthew 10:31, "Do not fear; therefore, you are of more value than many sparrows."

The Matthew Henry Bible commentary said, "Matthew chapter 10 is an ordination sermon, which Jesus preached when he ADVANCED his twelve disciples to the degree and dignity of apostles (promoted them to another level)." At this level, they could not be fearful for their lives. As we grow in Christ, we ought to come to a place where we no longer fear for our lives, no longer fear losing a job or dying, and no longer fear what people can do to us. A place where we no longer fear losing what we have and a place where we no longer fear potential sickness. A life that has matured in Christ is a life without fear.

Jesus sent His disciples on a special mission with particular instructions. In these directives, we discover the details of how to live fear-free, but before dispelling these valuable emotional nuggets, let's talk about things that provoke fear in us.

Talking to the lost about being found

Go to the lost sheep of the house of Israel" (Matthew 10:6, WEB). It can be intimidating to tell a sinner about getting saved when they think they are having the time of their life. Many people in the world are not ready to be converted. If committing adultery is wrong, if impure thoughts are wrong, if using people with sinister motives is wrong, and if un-forgiveness is wrong, they do not want to be right.

Jesus told them where to go (go to the lost sheep of Israel). So, they knew where to go and what to do. However, knowing where to go and what to do is one thing, but having the nerves to do it is another thing. The Jews, many of whom didn't like Jesus, wouldn't be so kind to His followers. Many people fear being scorned, ridiculed, or made fun of, which makes carrying out Jesus' commands challenging to say the least.

Jesus didn't send the disciples to the Gentiles; He sent them to fellow Jews. Sometimes another fear we have is having to share the gospel with a sibling because they know us better than anyone else, and often people who know much about us find it difficult to accept what we have to offer. Jesus once said a prophet has no honor in his hometown.

Barely getting by

Take no bag for your journey and do not take two coats or shoes or a stick: for the workman has a right to his food (Matthew 10:9-10a, BBE)

Jesus told them not to take certain things with them, but the things He told them not to take were things they needed daily such as money, shoes, clothes, and staff. We know why they needed money, clothes, and shoes, but what was the purpose of the staff? The staff kept them from falling when they traveled across the rugged mountains of Palestine. Jesus told them not to take money or clothes. He would provide food and clothing and not take a staff because He would keep them from falling. They could lean on Jesus.

In verse nine, Jesus taught His followers that they must cast away all cares that may hinder them from accomplishing the mission of God. If you are afraid of not having enough or losing things, then forget about being a Christian because this may happen sometimes. Faithful Christians will not let this bother them because they know God said in Genesis 15:1b: "...Fear not, Abram, I am your shield and your exceeding great reward." We should not be afraid because God is our shield and EXCEEDING GREAT REWARD.

God is our best, priceless possession, and if we lose anything, it shouldn't matter that much because it's all less than the God we possess. Your car may be worth $50,000, your savings account may be worth $150,000, and your house may be worth $350,000, BUT YOUR GOD is PRICELESS!

Some translations say of Genesis 15:1, "...your reward shall be great." The point is if you serve the Lord, rewards are certain.

Some people are afraid to obey the Lord because they think they will go lacking somehow or may have to give up too much. When we deny ourselves and endure our crosses, we experience lack, rejection, and various forms of persecution and other inconveniences. Still, to survive, we must keep in the forefront of our minds that God is faithful and will meet every need. Jesus taught His disciples a lesson on faith when He sent them out with nothing but the clothes on their backs. They had to learn to trust God to meet their needs. I believe God is trying to teach us this same lesson. Therefore, there may be times He may subtract things from our lives and lower the bank account to learn to rely on Him to meet every need so that we spend our time trying to do what He called us to do. I believe this is one reason why most people are not rich. God knows they will rely on wealth if they have it, so He doesn't make them rich, so they will learn to depend on Him instead.

The last part of verse 10 said: "...for the laborer is worthy of his food." Jesus told His disciples not to worry about what they did not have, but since they obeyed Him, what they needed would come to them. To labor means to put forth an effort. So, if you don't put forth an effort to do God's will but instead spend most of your time worrying about and chasing after material things, you may not get what God promised.

We don't have to fear not having our needs met. All we have to do is be faithful in serving God, and He will miraculously supply.

Rejection

And if anyone will not receive you or listen to your words, shake off the dust from your feet as you leave that house or town (Matthew 10:14, RSV)

Jesus taught His disciples how to deal with rejection. The fear of rejection is one of the primary motivations for doing what we do. We fear rejection because most of us validate our existence based on the acknowledgment of others, which is why Jesus Christ wants to be our best friend for life. In Christ, you will always have the support you need. I am with you always, even to the end of the age. Amen (Matthew 28:20, NKJV). Jesus promised never to forsake you. Then Jesus said, "Amen," which means so be it or it is so ordered. His presence will always be with us, and that is a guarantee.

The following will help us deal with rejection better. Remember that Jesus is perfect, and those who reject you are sinners just like you. So, when people reject you, say to yourself, you aren't anybody anyway, but a sinner just like me. You are not Jesus, so; your rejection doesn't mean that much. Always keep this in mind.

When Jews would return from a foreign country, they would shake the foreign dust off their feet to not pollute the holy land. Thus, when Jesus told His disciples to shake the dust off their feet of unbelieving Jews, those Jews were un-holy like the Gentiles. As a child of the highest God, you always have an advantage over those who are not saved, so when they reject the gospel, don't feel bad because all they are doing is keeping themselves in darkness and brokenness. But you are walking in the light and enjoying spiritual blessings in heavenly places. You don't have to do many activities to make yourself content because you have the Holy Spirit on the inside, and you are learning to be content in all circumstances.

Finally, verse 14 indicates that it may not be for you to win that person to Christ, and you may never be able to win them to Christ, but that doesn't mean that God doesn't have someone else in mind who can convince them to accept Christ. So, just because you shake the dust off of your feet regarding them, God will always have someone else to come along to share Christ with them. You will plant the seed of the gospel, another will water that seed, and another will do the reaping in due season. Just because people reject the gospel message, Christians should not faint but keep spreading the word.

When you appear weak

See, I send you out as sheep among wolves. Be then as wise as snakes and as gentle as doves (Matthew 10:16, BBE). I can only imagine what the disciples thought when Jesus told them He was sending them out as sheep among wolves. He already limited their belongings (Don't take anything extra). How much more vulnerable could they possibly be? On the surface, it appears that Jesus set them up for failure. Here is what sheep among wolves look like: When you forgive a person, who has treated you wrong, you look weak in the eyes of the world. When you are kind to those who mistreat you, you look vulnerable to the world. When you always give to others, and no one gives to you, you look weak in the eyes of the world. Although Jesus sent them out as sheep among wolves, He had already empowered them (Matthew 10:1). So, they may have appeared weak, but they were full of Holy Ghost's miraculous working power. Jesus wanted them to be humble, so He used the terms doves and sheep but bore in mind the meek shall inherit the earth (Matthew 5:5). We are not weak by a long shot. I like the words of the Apostle Paul, who says, "So I take pleasure in being feeble, in unkind words, in needs, in cruel attacks, in troubles, on account of Christ: for when I am feeble, then am I strong" (2 Corinthians 12:10, BBE).

On another occasion, Paul said, "Troubles are round us on every side, but we are not shut in; things are hard for us, but we see a way out of them; we are cruelly attacked, but not without hope; we are made low, but we are not without help. (2 Corinthians 4:8-9 BBE)." In other words, we are like the Ever-Ready Bunny; despite tribulation, we keep on going and going. The fact that we endure trials is proof that we are not weak.

Why Satan wants Christians to live in fear? To keep people in sin

Heal the sick, raise the dead, cleanse lepers, cast out demons. You received without paying, give without pay. (Matthew 10:8, RSV). If you don't share the gospel, sinners will not get saved because this is the only method by which soul conversion occurs. Had the disciples allowed fear to hinder them from doing what Jesus instructed, then many people would have remained in sin and bondage.

But how are men to call upon him in whom they have not believed? And how are they to believe in him of whom they have never heard? And how are they to hear without a preacher (Romans 10:14, RSV)? People cannot call upon what they have not believed, and they cannot believe in what they have not heard. Someone has to tell them about Jesus, and if Christians do not share the gospel, then sinners will not be saved. Still, we can rest assured that the world and Satan will guarantee the engulfment of people with deceptive, false doctrines and false religions, which will keep people ensnared in sin because Jesus is the only authentic way to God (John 14:6). Christians have the power to set men free, which is why Satan wants God's people to live in fear and reluctant to share the gospel because he knows Christians are the only ones who have what it takes to truly set men free and put them in right relationship with God. There is another reason why Satan wants Christians to live in fear.

To keep people suffering

There is another reason why Satan wants Christians to live in fear. Jesus endowed His disciples with the power to heal the sick and cast out demons, but fear can prevent this from happening. Unfortunately, many of our churches are spiritual kindergarten stations for carnal-minded Christians with itching ears. Sadly, many hirelings are eager to appease them, but the collateral damage is devastating. Many Christians never grow; they rarely pray except when they are in need and hardly ever fast. As a result, they lack the power to heal the sick and cast out demons. The very idea of doing so frightens me immensely.

People in need often followed Jesus because they knew He had what it took to heal them. Our churches need to step it up in the spiritual disciplines of prayer and fasting so our churches will become healing stations for hurting people to run to for restoration. Many parishioners are satisfied with doing nothing as long as they attend worship service. The preacher says some nice encouraging words that do not offend their lazy Christian lifestyles, then all is well in their world, but this will not save lost souls; it will not heal the sick and is certainly no threat to the Kingdom of Satan. The Devil is all about pain, oppression, possession, and death. Jesus once spoke of false prophets and false religions. "The thief comes only to steal and kill and destroy; I came that they may have life and have it abundantly." (John 10:10 RSV) If Satan can manipulate Christians to function in fear, people will continue to live a poor quality of life. Some people are wealthy but have a poor quality of life because they live outside of Christ. As Christians, we can't afford to live in fear because we are the light the world needs and the salt that will help save and preserve the people of this world.

Why Christians do not have to live in fear?

1. Jesus gave us authority

And he called to him his twelve disciples and gave them authority over unclean spirits, to cast them out, and to heal every disease and every infirmity (Matthew 10:1, RSV). Notice the words, "He gave them power/authority" The Greek word for authority or power is exousia, which means mastery or total control. We have complete control over demons to cast them out and heal the sick. The Greek word for power here also means superhuman. So, when we encounter demons, they are not just facing humans, but instead, they meet superhumans because Jesus gave us authority. The Greek word for power is also defined as a right. It is our right as Christians to cast out demons and heal the sick. Therefore, we have no reason to fear the powers of darkness because we have what it takes to overcome evil by doing good. Do not be overcome by evil, but overcome evil with good (Romans 12:21, RSV).

I find it most interesting that the meaning of the disciples' names reflects the power given them by Christ.

Peter means rock: We don't have to live in fear because we have Christ, the solid rock we stand.

Andrew means strong man: We are strong in the Lord and the power of His might (Ephesians 6:10).

John means the grace/mercy of the Lord: Surely goodness and mercy follows us everywhere we go, especially in times of trouble.

Philip means warlike: We are soldiers of the cross, fighting against spiritual darkness. Jesus is our Commander and Chief with all power, so the battle is won.

Judas (Judah) and Thaddeus mean praise: As we face the challenges, we do so with praise.

Simon means he hears and obeys: We do what the word of God says regardless of the consequences.

Matthew means the gift of the Lord: We offer the gift of salvation to the lost.

Not only do we have the power of God, but the fact that we are children of God gives us yet another reason not to live in fear.

2. We belong to Jesus

He called to himself HIS TWELVE DISCIPLES (Matthew 10:1, WEB). We are in the highest-ranking family in the entire universe, the family of God. Our daddy owns everything, and He can do all things, so it's irrational for us to fear anything and anybody.

3. As followers of Jesus Christ, the point is that we have the power to defeat the works of the enemy and set men free. The fact of our salvation is proof that we don't have to live in fear. For you did not receive the spirit of slavery to fall back into fear, but you have received the spirit of sonship when we cry, "Abba! Father" (Romans 8:15, RSV). We

have a spirit of freedom because where the spirit is, there is liberty, and we are no longer in bondage to fear. As adopted children of God, we can call Him daddy, and our daddy is in control of everything, so we have no need to worry about anything.

4. God sees all that is happening to you

Therefore, don't be afraid of them, for there is nothing covered that will not be revealed; and hidden that will not be known. (Matthew 10:26, WEB).

Never feel like God has forgotten you just because your enemies cause you problems because one day, God will uncover the truth, and people will know the truth, which is what happened to Job, whose friends accused him of wrongdoing. God sees your hurts, and He has a set time to rectify everything concerning you, and He will expose those who have tried to hurt your character under the pretense of truth-telling.

5. People cannot destroy your soul

Don't be afraid of those who kill the body but are not able to kill the soul. Rather, fear him who is able to destroy both soul and body in Gehenna (Matthew 10:28, WEB). The body is temporary and not meant to last forever, but the soul will last forever. It's better to die a temporal (bodily) death than an eternal (soul) death. So, if man destroys your body, he is not destroying the real you. The real you is the spirit inside of a fleshly shell. The soul is eternal, and only God can destroy the soul by casting it into hell.

The Apostle Paul put the icing on the cake regarding this subject; he writes, "For to me to live is Christ, and to die is gain" (Philippians 1:21, WEB).

We are of good courage, I say, and are willing rather be absent from the body and to be at home with the Lord (2 Corinthians 5:8, WEB). If someone kills your body, they will be doing you a favor by fast-tracking you into the presence of Jesus Christ.

6. God cares about the small things in your life

Are not two sparrows sold for a penny? And not one of them will fall to the ground without your Father's will. But even the hairs of your head are all numbered. Fear not; therefore, you are of more value than many sparrows (Matthew 10:29- 31, RSV).

A sparrow is about six inches long and weighs about an ounce. They are tiny birds. In Jesus' day, two sparrows were only worth a penny and of little value, but if they fell dead on the ground, God took notice of their death. Jesus is simply showing how much God cared for the disciples. Then Jesus went on to say that God knows how many hairs are on our heads. Nothing about you is too small in God's eyes. God is concerned about everything you do, how you feel, and what is best for you. So, if you face a huge problem, then indeed, God sees and cares about what is happening to you. God cares about small things in your life then; certainly, He cares about significant challenges.

The disciples had no reason to fear because God cared so much for them, and if He notices little cheap dead birds, indeed He cares for His disciples. "Look at the birds of the air: they neither sow nor reap nor gather into barns, yet your heavenly Father feeds them. Are you not of more value than they" (Matthew 6:26 RSV)? We are worth more than cheap sparrows because we are made in God's image, and in addition to this, we are Christians who are doing His will; therefore, God obligates Himself to take care of us.

As I draw to the close of Matthew chapter ten, there are a few more observations I will highlight.

Jesus makes wars not stars

A disciple is not above his teacher, nor a servant above his master (Matthew 10:24 RSV). We must not expect different treatment than Christ. We like to be adored and loved. I am sure Jesus' followers loved it when people called Him teacher, when He healed the sick, and when the crowds flocked behind Him. What about when Jesus was ridiculed, scorned, and called the god of manure? What about the times when His disciples betrayed, denied, and deserted Him when it was time for the cross? Jesus didn't do miracles to become a star. He came into the world to SERVE, SAVE, and SACRIFICE His life. Even as the Son of man came not to be served but to serve and give his life as a ransom for many (Matthew 20:28, RSV). Jesus makes wars, not stars!

There are no stars in the Kingdom of Christianity, only servants. When God blesses Christians to do something great, it is not to make them stars but glorify God and serve others. Let your light so shine before men, that they may see your good works and give glory to your Father who is in heaven (Matthew 5:16, RSV). Your service and accomplishments do not make you a star but rather point others to the true star, who is God. Everything you have and any talent you possess comes from God and belongs to Him. So, when people praise you, always give God the glory because Jesus is the real star.

But Jesus called them to him and said, you know that the rulers of the Gentiles lord it over them, and their great men exercise authority over them. It shall not be so among you, but whoever would be great among you must be your servant, and whoever would be first among you must be your slave (Matthew 20:25-27, RSV). The world's system is set up to lord it over others, but Jesus said those who are more blessed must serve others rather than others serving them. Notice Jesus said not so among you. We must not seek positions to rule over others, but we should seek to SERVE OTHERS. In Jesus' book, you are first when you serve instead of being served. Jesus is not in the business of making stars. Therefore, Christians must be careful not to get caught up in awards and worldly accolades that glorify people rather than God. Award shows such as the Oscars, Tony Awards, Grammy's, and yes, even some gospel award shows have very little to do with glorifying God; it's primarily about celebrating human effort.

If you have genuinely denied yourself and bear your cross, chances are you will not be popular. Suppose you are a Christian musician or singer that does not excessively water down the gospel in your lyrics, then don't expect to be hearing from the Grammys anytime soon. By the way, God does not need your help to relate to people in any time frame, modern or ancient. His gospel is powerful enough in its present form to touch lives (Romans 1:16) without all of the watered-down manipulations to lure fans, finances, and accolades. I listen to gospel music and contemporary Christian music, and often I sense 90% of glorified human experiences and 10% of the gospel. If we become like the world, we cannot truly transform it. Thank God for some Christian artists who remain faithful to the gospel message without the excessive carnal antics that make it hard to distinguish what is Christian and what is not. Some Christian artists try too hard to relate when as stated earlier, the gospel has the power to draw and change lives in its present state. We don't need to keep watering down the gospel; we need to fully commit to Christ in prayer, fasting, and using our spiritual gifts, and the Lord will effectively shine forth in this dark world.

What has brought the church to the point of trying schemes and different programs year after year to reach people? We do not have enough faith in the gospel itself, so we feel like we have to help God out. By the way, I believe that when churches arrange schemes to draw people, chances are if it takes manipulation to draw some people, I wonder what kind of people they are? If a scheme draws a person, then it is no wonder churches are full of carnal-minded ineffective laughing stocks of Satan. Suppose evangelists hit the streets like they are supposed to and preach the unadulterated gospel. In that case, lives will change, and churches will not have to overly concern themselves with human-made ideas to manipulate people to the church. Evangelism (preaching the good news on the highways and byways) is the key to earnest church growth, sinners coming to Christ rather than church hoppers who join because they heard the church had a great youth program. We have not been very serious about evangelism, and church flight is proof. Some churches uproot and move to better neighborhoods to attract and proselytize to maintain a particular culture while blatantly overlooking those who need their help the most. Churches do not need to relocate to the suburbs; they need to reach out and share Christ with those around them. We are so amazed at some of these large congregations that have built exquisite ecclesiological edifices after deserting the least of these. While some large churches (towers of babel) impress people, they do not enthrall God. Jesus spent most of His time ministering to the least of these because, quite frankly, they needed Him the most. The sinners, the poor, and those at the bottom of the barrel need a physician.

Just as some Christian musicians have ambiguously compromised the gospel, I believe some churches have done the same. If most churches were not desperately concerned about losing members and money, they would be free to preach the whole Bible, covering all subjects, both encouraging and offensive. They would avoid spending most of their time preaching the itching ear stuff that is sure to keep the nominal church folk in the pews. Jesus is not in the business of making stars; He makes wars. "Do not think that I have come to bring peace on earth; I have not come to bring peace, but a sword." (Matthew 10:34 RSV) In other words, all sorts of oppositions follow the preaching of the gospel. As you live for Christ and share His word and profess His standards, there will be times you will not be popular and admired. There will be times you look like a narrow-minded, intolerant Bible-thumping jerk. We should not expect to be loved because what we represent and the message we bring is not pretty in the eyes of ugly sin. After all, the world loves darkness rather than light.

We should be worried if people never have anything negative to say about us because Jesus said people spoke well of fake prophets in the Old Testament. Still, if you are genuinely committed to Christ, you cannot avoid worldly criticism. The gospel divides families because some resist it. A man will be hated by those of his house (Matthew 10:36, BBE). There will be times when people may not like you, but always remember Jesus makes wars, not stars.

Affliction is one sure thing that validates you as a Christian. He who does not take his cross and follow me is not worthy of me. He who finds his life will lose it, and he who loses his life for my sake will find it (Matthew 10:38, 39 RSV).

Christianity is not for Cowards

*Can't rely on money (Matthew 10:9, 10): There may be times when your bank account is low, but you always have Jehovah Jireh, your provider. In October 2008, the stock market crashed, and people lost large sums of money. Christ taught His disciples that they must learn to rely on Him and not depend on uncertain riches.

*Must learn to accept change (Matthew 10:11): Christ and his disciples were itinerant preachers. They took the gospel from city to city, which bespeaks constant change; we must not fear change. For in change, God brings about new things and new life.

*Can't feed on the acceptance of others (Matthew 10:14): Learn to shake off rejection and keep on moving. Do not depend on people to validate existence and service. You are a Christian, and Satan will use people to overturn your Christian service.

*Can't be afraid to speak up for Christ (Matthew 10:18): There will be times when you will be put on the spot to witness for Jesus, and you cannot let fear cause you to discredit the gospel by not standing up for Christ. If you are willing to stand up, the Holy Spirit will speak up through you: When they deliver you up, do not be anxious about how you are to speak or what you are to say; for what you are to say will be given to you in that hour (Matthew 10:19, RSV).

You must be willing to suffer. If you are not willing to suffer, your Christianity and commitment to Christ are questionable. Remember, "He who doesn't take up his cross and follow after me, isn't worthy of me." (Matthew 10:38) The Greek word for cross is "stauros," which means a post. It implies exposure to death. It also means self-denial. If you are not willing to deny yourself and put others first, your Christianity is not credible. As a Christian, the self is always second. Paul said in Romans 12:10 that we should put others ahead of ourselves.

He who finds his life will lose it, and he who loses his life for my sake will find it (Matthew 10:39, RSV). Jesus is saying just in case you decide not to deny yourself and not sacrifice your life for Him, then you will not save your life because you will lose in life one way or another. You may forsake God to seek worldly riches and pleasure, but you will eventually feel unfulfilled inside, rich but unfulfilled.

Your life becomes a blessing to others when you learn to live fear free

He who receives you receives me, and he who receives me receives him who sent me. He who receives a prophet because he is a prophet shall receive a prophet's reward, and he who receives a righteous man because he is a righteous man shall receive a righteous man's reward (Matthew 10:40; 41, RSV).

If the disciples had been afraid to do what Jesus told them, they would not have gone among the lost, and other people would not have had a chance to connect with Jesus. Notice He said whoever is kind to His disciples is kind to Him. My point is that the disciples did not allow fear to stop them from doing what Jesus told them to, and as a result, they became a blessing to others.

CHAPTER 2

Weathering Storms without Fear

In this chapter, we will reflect upon some nuggets shown me by the Holy Spirit about Matthew 14:23-33.

The disciples were on the Sea of Tiberias, which was about 10 miles wide, and the disciples were about four miles from the shore, which meant they were in the middle of the sea. But the boat was now in the middle of the sea, distressed by the waves, for the wind was contrary (Matthew 14:24, WEB). Imagine that they were in the middle of the sea in a raging storm, and perhaps the waves were high, but the good thing is, according to Matthew 14:22, they were where Jesus had sent them, so Jesus had an obligation to rescue them when things got out of control. Perhaps they did all they could to, but verse 24 said the wind was contrary, which meant they were helplessly back and forth by the wind. Sometimes problems can be too much for you to handle yourself, and there's absolutely nothing you can do. The question is, since Jesus was the one who sent them in that direction, what was He doing while they were battling the storm? He went up into the mountain by himself to pray. When evening came, he was there alone (Matthew 14:23, WEB). Jesus was praying while His disciples were in a storm, and no doubt, He prayed for them, which is why the waves didn't overcome them. The Apostle Paul said it best, "Christ who died, yes rather, who was raised from the dead, who is at the right hand of God, who also makes intercession for us" (Romans 8:34, WEB).

I imagine that the Holy Spirit led Jesus to meet His disciples since a storm had arisen, so it is good to be prayerful. The Holy Spirit will show you where you need to be.

God knew the disciples were in a storm because He permits storms, and when Jesus prayed, God notified Jesus about it, and He went to meet them. No matter what you face, no matter how horrible it seems, keep in mind that Jesus will meet you in your storm, mainly if you belong to Him.

Verse 26 says that the disciples cried out in fear when they saw this ghost-like figure approaching them, walking on water. They knew that no human could walk on water, so they thought it was a ghost. As they cried out in fear, they probably felt helpless because they had no control over the boat, and even worse, a spirit approached them. What they perceived to be an additional threat was their saving grace. Sometimes it's hard to see the Lord clearly when we face trouble, and we sometimes question if the Lord is near. Occasionally God moves in our problems, but we can't see Him due to fear; all we see is the storm and additional potential threats.

Interestingly one definition for Tiberias is "good vision." So, what the disciples saw on the Sea of Tiberias was not an impaired vision but a good vision; it was Jesus on His way to calm their storm. Sometimes supposedly, threats are blessings in disguise.

We will now focus on how Jesus uses tribulation to teach us not to fear.

Jesus speaks in our storms

But immediately, Jesus spoke to them, saying, "Cheer up! I AM! Don't be afraid" (Matthew 14:27, WEB). The first thing you need to notice about this verse is that before Jesus did anything about the storm, He immediately spoke comfort to His disciples because they were afraid. When we go through tough times, a word of comfort does a lot of good. "The Lord GOD has given Me the tongue of the learned, that I should know how to speak a word in season to him who is weary…" (Isaiah 50:4 NKJV)

Jesus told them to be of good cheer. In this text, the Greek word for cheer means to have courage which is the opposite of fear. God does not want us to be afraid when we face predicaments. Once again, Jesus spoke to them in the storm. Did Jesus yell or scream to them? The scripture doesn't say that, but we can assume that it was only natural that He yelled because of the noisy storm. Still, even if Jesus didn't scream, they heard His voice despite the hollowing winds and noisy waters. Just as Jesus supernaturally walked on water likewise, He could supernaturally make them hear His voice in the storm without Him having to raise His voice. I am sure the disciples didn't care how Jesus spoke to them in the storm as long as it was Jesus.

Jesus makes Himself known in our storms

The disciples were in a storm without Jesus, but it was Jesus who had sent them on ahead while He went to pray. As long as you are in God's will, you have nothing to fear because God is the One who sent you, and He will therefore manifest His power in times of trouble. The disciples had a very frightening situation. They were in the middle of a raging sea, but there was an additional unfortunate circumstance. Verse 25 said the storm occurred during the fourth watch, which means it was dark with poor visibility. In ancient times they divided the night into four-time frames. The first watch was from 6 pm to 9 pm; the second watch was from 9 pm to 12 midnight. The third watch was from 12 midnight to 3 am and the fourth watch was from 3 am to 6 am. When Christ came walking on water in the fourth watch of the night, it was between 3 am and 6 am. Perhaps the disciples thought their fate was sealed, and the sea would be their burial place. Indeed, Jesus would not be able to come to them because they were way out on the sea and it was dark, but to their surprise, their Savior showed up in the storm. Do not fear when you are in trouble because Jesus knows where you are, and He will come to you and make Himself known in your storm. I believe one reason Jesus permitted His disciples to experience the storm was so He could walk on water to prove to His disciples that no circumstance, regardless of how dangerous, can stop Him from getting to those who belong to Him. Jesus knew that His disciples were desperate, so His walking on the water showed His intensity and eagerness to help them. Jesus helps sinners, so what makes you think He would not put forth a special effort to come to the aid of His disciples in a time of need.

When Jesus showed up, He pulled rank and used the biggest title of all, indicating His authority and power. He said, "It is I" literally, I am. Jesus used this same language in John 8:58, where He said, "Before Abraham was I am," and in the Old Testament, I AM was used to refer to Jehovah (Exodus 3:14). So when Jesus said it is I, He said it is the Great "I AM," who is coming to you, the Almighty God who made the wind and the waves, the Almighty God who rules the wind and waves and makes them obey. Don't worry about the wind because I made it, and don't worry about the waves; I made them too, and since I made them, I also control them and tell them what to do.

Your problem may be out of your control, but it's under God's control. So, when your life is out of control, remember God still has everything under His control and will make it work for your good. God will make Himself known in your storm because you belong to Him.

Jesus invites us to walk by faith in our storms

And He said, Come. And when Peter had come down out of the boat, he walked on water to go to Jesus (Matthew 14:29, MKJV). Jesus invited Peter to come to Him amid a terrible storm. There was no bridge to cross over the water, so the other disciples had to think Peter was insane to step out of the boat. If you trust Jesus, He will awaken the spirit of power (2 Tim. 1:7) within you to do miracles. Jesus impaired the laws of gravity which was a manifestation of His infinite power. We have this same power available to us as Christians, so there is no reason to fear anything, and if we use faith more, we will become fearless. The storm was bigger than Peter physically, but he remained on top of it as long as he walked by faith. When we learn to live fear-free by walking in faith, we will find ourselves on top of our problems emotionally instead of them on top of us, which oppresses us psychologically, causing us to worry unnecessarily, thereby robbing us of peace and sleep. King Solomon addressed the issue of fear by encouraging us to trust the wisdom of God, and when we do so, we attain the peace of God. "Then you will go safely on your way, and your feet will have no cause for slipping. When you take your rest, you will have no fear, and on your bed, sleep will be sweet to you." (Proverbs 3:23; 24, BBE). Peter trusted what Jesus said, and as a result, he did something no other human being has done except Christ Himself. Faith and obedience to Jesus' word eliminate fear because when we obey and trust God, He works miracles in our lives which helps us feel secure. When you fail to walk by faith, fear will dominate your life. Without faith, it is impossible to learn to master your storms with the exclusion of fear.

Why didn't Jesus simply show up in their boat instead of walking towards them on the water? I believe He wanted to get their attention so they could see an example of faith. Jesus knows all things, and He knew they would be afraid. He also knew Peter would ask to join Him on the water, and the disciples would see a person like themselves walk by faith upon the stormy sea. Jesus wanted His disciples to see that anything is possible by faith and that they could be victorious in the middle of a storm and not just when it is overr.

Fear hinders us from experiencing miracles

But when he saw that the wind was strong, he was afraid and beginning to sink; he cried out, saying, Lord, save me (Matthew 14:30, WEB)! First of all, Peter was not the average disciple. He had something extra, a little more faith and slightly less fear. Peter trusted Christ more than the average disciple because he was the only one who agreed to step out of the boat (box) on the water just because Jesus said he could. Peter was the only one who went to trial with Jesus when the trouble started while the other disciples had run and hid. Peter was not an average disciple. He had great faith in walking on water, but he made the mistake of looking at the turbulent waves. As long as Peter kept his eyes on Jesus, he stayed afloat, but he began to sink when he started paying more attention to the problems around him. Fear hinders us from experiencing miracles. In Matthew 14:31, Jesus asked Peter why he doubted. Then He said Peter had little faith. If Peter had little faith, how much smaller was the faith of those who stayed in the boat? Generally speaking, many people have little faith in God. The Greek word for little faith here is oligopistos which means lacking confidence in Christ. Jesus asked Peter, why do you have so little confidence in Me? How do you handle adversity? Would Jesus ask you why you have such little trust in Him?

Jesus uses storms to help us get to know Him better

When they got up into the boat, the wind ceased. Those who were in the boat came and worshiped him, saying, you are truly the Son of God" (Matthew 14:32, 33 WEB)! Some people confuse knowing about Jesus with knowing Jesus. Many people know about Jesus, but they do not have an intimate relationship with Him. God uses trials to help us encounter Him more personally, which happened to the disciples in verse 33. We must exercise our faith in our trials to get to know Jesus better. Notice Peter could see Jesus better than the other disciples because he walked by faith towards Jesus in the storm while the others were aimlessly floating along at a standstill in the boat. But after Jesus got in the ship, up close and personal, and the storm ceased, the disciples said, "…Truly you are the Son of God." Didn't they know this already? Consider this: They saw Jesus turn water into wine, but now they saw an even more bizarre miracle. This time Jesus walked on water, and if that wasn't strange enough, He even invited Peter to walk on water also, and Peter did it. If the disciples had any doubt about who Jesus was, it was laid to rest when He and Peter walked on water. Jesus permitted the storm to help His disciples get to know Him deeper.

CHAPTER 3

How Favor Dissolves Fear

T his chapter will look at Mary's life to ascertain how an awareness of God's favor can purge fear from our lives. Luke writes, "The angel said to her, "Don't be afraid, Mary, for you have found favor with God" (Luke 1:30, WEB). When she heard this good news, it raised her anxiety level, according to verse 29. She wondered what the angel meant by highly favored. When Gabriel told her that she would give birth to the Christ child, she did not feel worthy, as reflected in verse 48. For he has had pity on his maidservant, though she is poor and lowly placed (Luke 1:48, BBE); this does not sound like a person who thinks highly of themselves and their circumstances. Some people find it challenging to accept great things because they don't feel worthy with such humble and meager backgrounds. Mary may not have felt worthy, but she readily accepted God's will, although something like this had never been done before and would never happen again. The angel told her she was highly favored, i.e., she would give birth to the Son of God. Mary would make history and be remembered for the duration of human existence until the second coming of Christ, which indeed was tremendous favor. Imagine how President Obama's mother would have felt if an angel had told her she would give birth to a man who would be president of the most powerful country in world history. It is honorable to give birth to sports legends, presidents, and world-renowned leaders, but Mary gave birth to the King of Kings and the Lord of Lords, the Son of Almighty God, and this is why the angel said Mary was highly favored above all women.

The angel said Mary found favor with God. Interestingly, Mary was not looking for favor; she lived her life looking forward to marrying her sweetheart, Joseph. She was not seeking status, but the life she lived pleased God, and as a result, favor found her, which is an excellent lesson for single people.

When they live holy and seek to be intimate with Christ, favor finds them. The spouse you have been wanting and the security you desire finds you, but when you aspire to be close with people but fail to get intimate with God first, usually the wrong people find you. When you seek things and people first, generally, disappointment will find you. Mary found favor with God based on the life she lived. There were many virgins in that culture, so God could have chosen anyone of them, but I believe it took more than simply being a virgin because virgins were typical during that time.

We catch a glimpse of Mary's character in verse 38. Mary said, "Behold, the handmaid of the Lord; be it to me according to your word." The angel departed from her (Luke 1:38, EB). Mary said yes to God, although it would bring about some tough challenges, starting with the man she was engaged to and loved. She would have to tell Joseph that she would have a baby, that the baby would not be his, and that God would be the father. Can you imagine what went through Joseph's mind? Most men would have thought Mary cheated, and to cover herself, she tried to use God and expect people to believe it was a miracle. If you were in the military and had to leave the country for a year, your wife tells you she is pregnant, and it's a miracle. You would probably say no, it's a man. Joseph intended to divorce Mary or intended to do so secretly. The angel didn't give Mary any instructions on explaining this to Joseph because the angel knew God already had that part covered, but this would not make it any easier for Mary when she would have to explain this to her fiancé. With this in mind, I am prone to think that some people would have rejected what the angel offered, but Mary was obedient to the will of the Lord. Therefore, the virgin God chose to give birth to the world's Savior and had a heart of obedience for God by choosing short-term embarrassment above her persona.

God expects us to obey Him no matter how difficult life may seem. He does not care about how we look in the eyes of others, nor does God care about what others think about what He told us to do. All God is concerned about is our obedience, and when we obey, He will manifest His will to those around us at some point and rectify all things. If you face difficult circumstances and your faith is tested like never before. Don't give up! Be like Mary and say, Lord, I am your servant, and may it be as you said. Favor finds you when you are willing to say yes to God amidst extreme problematic situations. Knowing she had God's blessing made it a little easier to be willing to accept a problematic short-term task. After Mary told Joseph, as expected, he doubted at first, but later God, who is faithful, revealed the truth to Joseph in a dream.

The results of favor combat fear

When Mary discovered that she had the favor of God, it ignited happiness in her life; it affirmed her faith and added passion to her praise, all of which diminished fear. Luke writes, "Blessed is she who believed" (Luke 1:48a, WEB). The Greek word for blessed is Makarios, which means supremely blessed, but it means happy or happier by extension. Mary had every reason to be happy because of God's promises, and her happiness quenched her fears.

Mary said, happy is she that believed. She believed God was going to fulfill His promise. Therefore, she had no reason to fear. I heard it said that when faith is high, fear is low, but when trust is low, anxiety is high. If you can muster up enough faith in God, you will feel more at ease. But whoever listens to me will dwell securely and be at ease, without fear of harm (Proverbs 1:33 WEB).

She was overwhelmed by God's favor in her life; she could not contain her praise. Mary said, "My soul magnifies the Lord. My spirit has rejoiced in God my Savior. He has looked at the humble state of his handmaid. For behold, from now on, all generations will call me blessed" (Luke 1:46-48, WEB). Mary was so happy and grateful that the Lord showed her favor by choosing her to give birth to the world's Savior that she erupted with heartfelt praise. I imagine Mary felt that nobody knew who she was until the Lord showed her favor, and now all generations after her will know who she is, and for that, she felt obligated to praise the Lord. She was a nobody until the Lord showed her favor, and now her name is a household name, and for that, she had to praise the Lord. Every Christmas season, people talk about her because there is no other woman on earth who can say their Son is the Savior of the world, and for that, she had no choice but to praise the Lord. She thought that God blessed her to give birth to the most incredible man in history in an animal stable and crucified on a cross of shame, but now her Son sits on the throne right next to God Himself, and for that, she had to praise the Lord.

CHAPTER 4

Reasons Why We Shouldn't Fear

In this chapter, we will look at certain things that we can do to make it difficult to worry. Jesus' life and words unveil four secrets to living fear-free.

It's difficult to fear when you:
Are in God's will

In Mark 4:1-34, Jesus had been doing God's will, and now He sought well-earned repose in the stern of the boat despite a storm. He could relax even in the storm because He was in the will of God. Some people live in fear because they are not in God's will, or they fear because they know God's will but do not obey. And a great windstorm arose, and the waves beat into the boat so that it was already filling (Mark 4:37, NKJV). Imagine the waves hitting against the boat and water was filling up in the boat. I can visualize the disciples seeing the water on the boat's floor as it slowly rose to their ankles and eventually escalated to near their knees, and all of a sudden, they yelled, "Jesus, can we a little help here? You help everybody else, and now are you going to let your disciples drown?"

Remember that when you do God's will, the Devil will cause disturbances to discourage you and hopefully stop you from carrying out God's plan. Jesus and His disciples had just finished ministering to a crowd of people, and as soon as He tried to get some rest, a storm arose. I have often said that if you are indeed the salt of the earth and the light of the world, you are a prime target of Satan, and every chance he gets, he will cause a storm in your life. The point is Jesus was asleep with His head resting on a pillow in the back of the boat. I looked up more details about the vessel's stern and found two interesting things.

*The stern is built over a part of the boat, a structural beam over which the ship's back end is built. As you know, a structural beam holds things up. Jesus was in God's will, and no matter how bad the storm was, God was holding them up.

*People who canoe often say the stern of the boat is the position from which the navigation of the canoe is done. The person in the front of the canoe generates the power. However, the disciples were in front of the boat had no control in the storm. Jesus, who controls all things, was in the back of the boat sleeping like a baby in the storm. You may be in the front of the boat of your life, but you are not in control. Jesus may be silent in your circumstances, but He is still in charge. You can enter God's rest even when life throws you a curveball when you do God's will. Are you in God's will? If so, then you have no reason to fea.

You have no reason to fear when:
You have accepted the word of God

Then He arose and rebuked the wind and said to the sea, "Peace, be still!" And the wind ceased, and there was a great calm (Mark 4:39,

NKJV). Here we see that Jesus' words have the power to change situations. Notice the words, "...there was a great calm." The Greek word for great is Megas which means a massive amount of peace. What is interesting about the word Megas figuratively speaking means to fear exceedingly in an extensive application. It is as if the storm which caused the disciples to be afraid became afraid when Jesus spoke to it. If we live by the word of God, we will avoid living in unnecessary fear because God's word has the power to change conditions.

In verse 35, Jesus had already told them they were going to the other side, and since His word has power, that is what would happen. We need to accept what He said and not focus on how the condition of our surroundings. Always remember circumstances may change, but God's word stays the same, and it's going to be just like He said. In verse 39, Jesus didn't have to speak to the wind because He had already told His disciples about what would happen in verse 35. If Jesus spoke and made the wind obey, when He said they were going to the other side, His word would push them through the storm until they reached the other side.

Some church folk may never reach the other side to experience the miracles of God because they have not truly accepted the word of God. The disciples believed in Jesus because they followed Him, and they trusted to a degree what He said, but the storms often revealed that the disciples had not entirely accepted what Jesus said. We can have a fundamental belief in God's word, but we must accept them wholeheartedly to experience Jesus on a whole new level. James 2:19 says, if you believe, then that's fine, but even demons believe, but we know demons do not accept God's word into their lives. Some church folk believe but have not received God's word or integrated it into their daily living, explaining how some folk can be in church for years and stay the same. The problem was the disciples forgot what

Jesus had said in verse 35. Fear keeps many people from standing on God's word and missing their miracles, but when we accept God's word into our lives, it empowers us in times of trouble. God's word empowers us to avoid the grip of fear.

You have no reason to fear when you know that: Jesus never leaves you

But He was in the stern, asleep on a pillow. And they awoke Him and said to Him, "Teacher, do You not care that we are perishing" (Mark 4:38, NKJV). He was in the boat with the disciples. He was not coming toward them walking on water in this instance, but He was already in the boat. The disciples had a problem with Jesus, although He was in the boat. Jesus was not saying and doing anything, but He, the Master of the sea, did not have to do anything. He is the Son of God, and thus His heavenly Father had them covered. Because of who Jesus is, He did not have to do anything; all He had to do was be present. Do not fear because God is silent and does not seem to be doing anything, although your life is falling apart. Jesus is in the boat with you; the power source is on the scene even though the storm rages on, but Jesus is in control, and everything is alright.

I looked at some things Jesus had done before Mark chapter 4 and found that in Mark chapter 1, Jesus had cast out an evil spirit, healed Peter's mother-in-law, and cleansed a leper.

In Mark chapters two and three, Jesus preached, taught, and healed people. Therefore, in Mark chapter 4, the disciples should have known better than worry because they had the miracle worker in the boat. They knew God was with Jesus, and since Jesus was with them in the storm, they were fated to be alright. David Brenner, a famous comedian in the nineteen seventies, once told about when he was on a plane and a torrential storm arose. An old lady prayed in the seat in front of him. "Lord, I am not worried because I know I am in the palm of your hands," she said. At that point, David Brenner said he felt comfortable because if that old lady who sat in front of him was in the palm of God's hand, then surely, he must be on God's risk, he thought. If we have Christ in our lives, we should not fear when trials come because He never leaves us.

The disciples rushed ahead of God by waking Jesus up, but I wonder what kind of miracle God would have done had they just by faith waited on God since God's only Son was in the boat with them. Some folk rush ahead of God and never discover what He had in store concerning their situation. The disciples focused intensely on the storm and forgot who they had in the boat with them. They made the problem more extensive than the problem solver. As long as Jesus is with us, let the winds blow. So what? We got Jesus. I would have done like little children do when thunder thumps and lightning flashes. They run and get in the bed with their parents. If I were in the boat with the disciples, I would have laid down beside Jesus during the storm.

The next time you have a storm in your life, try to remember to cuddle up with Jesus in prayer. He may not say anything back to you, but you know He's there because He promised to be with us until the end of this age. I like the way the Book of Job addresses the issue of not living in fear; it says, "You will lie down, and none will make you afraid; many will entreat your favor" (Job 11:18 RSV).

You have no reason to fear if:
Your faith is maturing

The wind fell, and there ensued a great calm. Then he said to them: Why are you so afraid? Have you still no faith (Mark 4:40, MNT)? In other words, Jesus said, after all the things you have seen Me do, do you still have no faith? God has brought us through some incredible trials and tight situations where we didn't know how we were going to pull through, but by the grace of God, we made it. Perhaps His question resonates with us: do you still not have faith, after all, I have done for you?

The disciples had a storm, but they also had Jesus. They knew where Jesus was, and they certainly knew where the storm was, but the question is, where was their faith? You may know about Jesus, but this will not make a difference if you don't have faith in times of trials.

The disciple's lack of faith did not come as a surprise to Jesus. He knew where their faith level was all along. So, what was Christ trying to do? He permitted the storm to see where their faith was to improve their loyalty. Without faith, it is impossible to please God, and if God is not pleased, we will not have power, and without power, the storms of life will grant us inevitable defeat. Jesus wanted His disciples to grow in faith, which is why I believe He didn't rush to do something right away. He had done enough miracles by then for them to be well assured that all they had to do was trust God, and something would happen even if Jesus remained asleep in the stern.

Some of your storms are not by chance but by divine order to help your faith mature, so you don't have to live in fear when you have undesirable and threatening situations.

CHAPTER 5

Resurrection, the Primary Reason to Not Fear

We have discussed numerous reasons we should not live in fear. However, this chapter offers the most crucial motivation not to let fear dominate our lives. But now Christ is risen from the dead (1 Corinthians 15:20, NKJV). Paul went on to say, "For "He has put all things under His feet" (1 Corinthians 15:27, NKJV). Christ the Lord (Kurios) has supreme authority. He controls all things (Matthew 28:18). We are in Christ Jesus, who is omniscient and omnipotent; therefore, we can divorce ourselves from all fears because of who Jesus is. If Jesus did not rise from the grave, we would have every reason to fear, but we have no reason to worry since He rose from the dead.

We know these great truths, but why is it so hard to put them into practice? As Jesus' ministry was six months from closure, He told His disciples what His fate would be: "And they were in the way going up to Jerusalem. And Jesus went before them. And they were amazed, and as they followed, they were afraid. And he retook the twelve and began to tell them what would happen to Him, saying, Behold, we go up to Jerusalem. And the Son of man will be betrayed to the chief priests and the scribes. And they will condemn Him to death and deliver Him to the Gentiles. And they will mock Him, and will scourge Him, and will spit on Him, and will kill Him. And the third day He shall rise again" (Mark 10:32-34 MKJV).

Jesus left Galilee and made His way toward Jerusalem, fully aware that He would be challenged by many unfriendly opponents and tolerate an excruciating death. Therefore, the twelve disciples were amazed and afraid of what was before them. It is no wonder they all scattered during the trial of Christ and crucifixion.

What was the source of their fear?

The root of their fear came from having disregarded Jesus' itinerary for the twilight days of His earthly ministry. On numerous occasions, Jesus told the disciples the details of His fate. From that time, Jesus went on to make clear to his disciples how he would have to go up to Jerusalem, and undergo much at the hands of those in authority and the chief priests and scribes, and be put to death, and the third day come again from the dead (Matthew 16:21, BBE). Jesus reminded His disciples of this fact at least eight times (Matthew 20:17; Mark 8:31; 9:31; 10:33; Luke 9:22; 18:31; 24:6-7).

The first time Jesus announced His pending trial and crucifixion was about six months before His execution. Jesus did not tell them about the tribulation in store for Him early in His ministry because He did not want them to become discouraged. However, when He finally told them, they resisted. And Peter, protesting, said to him, "Be it far from you, Lord; it is impossible that this will come about" (Matthew 16:22, BBE). In essence, Peter said, 'You are the Son of God, but you must not go to the cross. The cross was not in their vocabulary, and the disciples fought it right up to the seizure of Christ. Peter did not accept God's plan (will) because he tried to stop the soldiers from taking Christ by cutting off the ear of one of the soldier.

Why the disciples could not grasp that Christ had to suffer?

It is crucial to remember that there were dual exhibitions of the Messiah in Jewish scripture. One was the suffering servant, and the other was the ruling King.

Isaiah 53:5 is a depiction of the Messiah as a suffering servant. Isaiah writes, "But it was for our sins he was wounded, and for our evil doings he was crushed: he took the punishment by which we have peace, and by his wounds, we are made well" (Isaiah 53:5, BBE).

Isaiah 9:6 is a depiction of the Messiah as the ruling King. He says, "For to us a child is born, to us, a son is given; and the government will be upon his shoulder, and his name will be called "Wonderful Counselor, Mighty God, Everlasting Father, Prince of Peace." (Isaiah 9:6, RSV).

The Disciples expected the Messiah, the ruling King, to unshackle Israel from Roman domination, which explains why on Palm Sunday, when Jesus entered the city riding a donkey colt, the people cried, Hosanna! The meaning of the word Hosanna is "save now." Therefore, when the crowd shouted the word Hosanna, they acknowledged Christ as their King and looked to him for immediate deliverance. Synonyms for Messiah are champion, liberator, defender, or savior. The disciples wanted their champion to save them instantly. They did not entertain the notion that the Messiah would come to suffer first and later reign as King in His Second Coming, which explains why they celebrated on Sunday when Jesus entered the city as King. Still, when they took Him into custody, the people lost interest because Jesus did not do what they thought He should do. So, it is understandable that some disappointed with Him cried crucify Him on Friday but had shouted Hosanna on Sunday. The people wanted deliverance and prosperity immediately, and when they did not get it, they felt justified to shout crucify the man who had raised their hopes to no avail.

The primary reason we do not have to live in fear (Mark 10:34)

They shall mock him, and shall spit upon him, and shall scourge him, and shall kill him; and after three days, he shall rise again (Mark 10:34, ASV). The first part of this verse incites fear in us, but the last part sustains our hope.

Jesus repeated numerous times that He was going to Jerusalem to die (Matthew 16:21; 17:12; 17:22-23; 20:18-29; 20:28), and at least three times, He said He would rise from the grave. Despite having told the disciples repeatedly that he would rise from the tomb on the third day, they failed to comprehend the implications thereof.

Afterward, he was revealed to the eleven themselves as they sat at the table, and he rebuked them for their unbelief and hardness of heart because they didn't believe those who had seen him after he had risen (Mark 16:14, WEB). In John 20:19-21, Jesus appeared to the disciples, and He spoke peace to them. The doors were closed and locked, but all of a sudden, Jesus appeared without using the door. Why did He make such an entrance? I believe He wanted to make sure the disciples got the message that He had risen from the grave. He tried to assure the disciples that He had risen indeed, and thus He walked through the wall making a grand entrance to solidify their trust.

In John 20:24-28, Thomas was not with them when Jesus first appeared to them, and when they told him they saw Jesus, he said he wouldn't believe until he placed his finger in the nail prints in Jesus' hands and the hole in His side. In John 20:26-28, a week later, the disciples locked themselves inside a room again, and this time Thomas was present, and Jesus showed up again. By the way, Jesus spoke peace to them again, why they were still locked up, hiding, and afraid. When Jesus showed up and saw Thomas, He told him to put his hand in His side. When the disciples told Thomas they saw Jesus; He was not present. Therefore, the second time Jesus showed up, it was to help Thomas exclusively. I believe God will do something special to reach an individual. Our Lord uttered a parable concerning a shepherd leaving ninety-nine sheep to find one lost sheep.

After seeing the nail prints, Thomas cried my Lord and my God (John 20:28). Notice Thomas said my Lord and my God. The word Lord is Kurios (controller-supreme authority). Thomas also called Jesus God (theos-supreme deity). When Thomas saw the resurrected Jesus, he saw more than just a King; He saw God in human form. A God in human form that made a personal trip a second time to convince him that He had risen indeed. Once Thomas laid eyes on Jesus, doubting Thomas became believing Thomas, and then he no longer had a reason to fear anything or anybody.

Jesus had to show the disciples that the suffering Messiah was not defeated. He showed them that the suffering Messiah is still the ruling King. Jesus' suffering didn't make Him any less a king. King's road horses, but when Jesus rode the donkey, it made Him no less a king.

Again Mark's Gospel says, "They shall mock him, and shall spit upon him, and shall scourge him, and shall kill him; and after three days he shall rise again" (Mark 10:34, ASV).

Jesus' enemies did all of these horrible things to Him and then had him crucified. It was not their intent for Him to bounce back from such extreme persecution and destruction, but to their dismay, on the third day, Jesus said, "I am back," and all of a sudden, His disciples saw that Jesus was a ruling King after all. They saw that Jesus had gotten the victory and that He was undeniably and reliably King of kings and the Lord of lords.

I imagine that when the disciples laid eyes on the resurrected Christ, nothing else He had ever done could even compare. Water to wine, walking on water, healing the sick, casting out demons, feeding five thousand with two fish and five loaves of bread could not even compare to when they laid eyes on resurrected Jesus, who rose from the grave without the assistance of any man. The disciples saw that everything Jesus said came to pass. When He rose again, they knew He had the victory over His enemies. They knew nothing, and nobody was more incredible than Jesus. Laying eyes on the resurrected Jesus transformed their thinking, and they went from being fearful and becoming fearless. Before the resurrection, the disciples were terrified, but after the resurrection, they were brave. They, therefore, departed from the presence of the council, rejoicing that they were counted worthy to suffer dishonor for Jesus' name (Acts 5:41, WEB). After the resurrection, the disciples were willing to suffer and rejoice in their suffering. They live fear-free despite intense persecution.

Here is a fact. We don't have to live in fear because Jesus, who is the controller of everything, rose from the grave, and we belong to Him. I like the way the Apostle Paul puts it, "Who is he who condemns? It is Christ who died, yes rather, who was raised from the dead, who is at the right hand of God, who also makes intercession for us" (Romans 8:34-35, 37-39, WEB). Jesus' resurrection is the key in this verse and is the foundation for the following verses. Not only is Jesus alive, but He is praying for us. If the prayers of the righteous saints are effective, then certainly Jesus' prayers are supremely potent and sufficient. With this in mind, we have no reason to fear.

No, in all these things, we are more than conquerors through him who loved us (Romans 8:37, WEB). The phrase "we are conquerors" means we have an indisputable, unquestionable, and overwhelming victory. Once again, given our new status in Christ Jesus, we have nothing to fear.

Many things listed in Romans 8:35, 38-39 cause fear. All these things can cause people to live in terror, but since we are in Christ who rose from the grave, we do not have to fear any of these things anymore because we are eternally joined with Christ. Nothing can separate us from God's love. Since God is love (1 John 4:8) and nothing can separate us from His love, nothing can separate us from God. The fact that we can never be separated from Christ dissipates all fear.

www.ingramcontent.com/pod-product-compliance
Lightning Source LLC
Chambersburg PA
CBHW031236120626
46545CB00003B/1152